MW00462322

Fine Lines

a celebration of
clothesline culture

Cindy Etter-Turnbull

Pottersfield Press, Lawrencetown Beach, Nova Scotia, Canada

Copyright © 2006 Cindy Etter-Turnbull

All rights reserved. No part of this publication may be reproduced or used or transmitted in any form or by any means – graphic, electronic or mechanical, including photocopying – or by any information storage or retrieval system, without the prior written permission of the publisher. Any requests for photocopying, recording, taping or information storage and retrieval systems of any part of this book shall be directed in writing to Access Copyright, The Canadian Copyright Licensing Agency, 1 Yonge Street, Suite 1900, Toronto, Ontario M5E 1E5 (www.accesscopyright.ca). This also applies to classroom use.

Library and Archives Canada Cataloguing in Publication

Etter-Turnbull, Cindy

Fine lines : a celebration of clothesline culture / Cindy Etter-Turnbull.

ISBN 1-895900-77-8

I. Title.

TT998.E87 2006   C813'.6   C2006-900149-9

Cover design by Dalhousie Design Services

Cover photo: Valarie Cunningham

Pottersfield Press acknowledges the ongoing support of The Canada Council for the Arts, and the financial support of the Government of Canada through the Book Publishing Industry Development Program for our publishing activities. We also acknowledge the support of the Nova Scotia Department of Tourism, Culture and Heritage.

Pottersfield Press
83 Leslie Road
East Lawrencetown
Nova Scotia, Canada, B2Z 1P8
Website: www.pottersfieldpress.com
To order, phone 1-800-NIMBUS9 (1-800-646-2879)
Printed in Canada

To my husband Chris
and children Jon and Nathan,
whose support provided me
the opportunity to follow my ambition.

Contents

Introduction

Clotheslines are one of the most practical tools ever created.

Clotheslines are

> useful,
> environmentally friendly,
> hypoallergenic,
> cheap to install,
> low in maintenance,
> long-lasting,
> safe,
> easy to operate,
> multifunctional,
> artistic,
> and peaceful.*

(* some exceptions may apply under less than optimal conditions)

We all agree, there is nothing fresher than bed sheets straight off the line. Their wholesome smell tempts you to shroud your body among their smooth, silky fabric. Crawling between line-dried sheets after a warm bath is absolutely blissful. Wake up! We have just started to discover all the hidden secrets and divine details of our beloved friend.

There is a sense of pride and self-satisfaction in hanging a line of laundry in such a way that pleases the eye. Our "lines" are meaningful scripts, narratives of innocence and charm. The common parallels between our lives and our lines are strikingly similar. Our symmetry of expression reflects our emotions and principles. Any piece of art is representative of original, personal style. Your line is as unique as you are. The bond created between you and your line is unmistakably a labour of love. While some of you may not have a clothesline of your own yet, others of you can relate to what I am saying.

Let's go back to the beginning . . . On a warm fall day when my husband and I were driving to our favourite fishing place, we drove past a particularly pleasing line of clothes. I commented, "Now there is a fine line."

Chris laughed and asked what made that line finer than all the others we had passed. I told him what set it apart. Continuing our drive, we assessed each passing line more attentively. Our discussion had ceased and we had started a game of finding the "best line" and it wasn't a fishing line.

Chris said he was fastened to the clothesline with a harness when he was a young boy because he kept venturing away. We laughed, shared more stories and agreed someone should write a book about clotheslines.

A few moments passed. We looked at each other. It suddenly dawned on me that not everyone understands the hidden secrets of a *fine line*. I recalled all the clothesline experiences I had as a child and with my own children. Then I realized I was smiling and it felt good. If I had such fond memories, I wondered if other people did too. I needed to find out and share the larger story. "Well," I said, "I'm not doing anything. Maybe that person could be me." And as simply as that I was on a book writing mission.

When I told my family I was going to write a book, they were very supportive. Chris provided me such freedom to explore my potential, I will always be grateful to him. My mother told me my father would be very proud of me and that is all anyone needs to hear to succeed.

I had to figure out a plan of action. The first thing I asked myself was, "What do I need to get started?" The answer was a basket of laundry, a questionnaire, a pen, a camera, and people – many knowledgeable people. Fortunately, I already had a desk and a computer. I did have to get another desk and a file cabinet before all was said and done.

I drafted some letters and sent them off to various organizations in the surrounding area, asking if they would be interested in participating in my project. The response from seniors groups, church groups, the local breast cancer survivor group, elementary schools, and private group interviews was overwhelming. If I wanted feedback from people they needed a way to contact me, so my son Jon created a business card with the caption "Mrs. Clothesline." If it weren't for my boys, Nathan and Jon, I'm not sure I could have gotten past the technological side of things.

The first interview I ever conducted was with a seniors group – The Rawdon Golden Youth in Rawdon, Nova Scotia. It was January 20, 2003, and we had agreed if the roads were bad the event would be cancelled. In the back of my mind, I was hoping it would storm. Standing up in front of a group of strangers who knew more about life than I, left me feeling alone and thinking maybe I should reconsider this venture. After all, *they* already knew everything there was to know about clotheslines. There were eleven people gathered at the hall that afternoon, eight ladies, two gentlemen and me. Never having done such a thing before, you can appreciate how nervous I was. I didn't know any of these people. What if they thought this whole idea was foolish and a waste of time, *their* time?

The moment came. I stood up, told them this was the first interview I'd conducted and I was nervous. Then I began to tell them a bit about myself and my reason for writing this book. Once we began to interact, we all loosened up and the fun began. I started to ask them questions about their clotheslines and how they hung their laundry. I was on my way.

I collected the information I wanted on a questionnaire. Each item in my basket was on the sheet. I would ask how you would hang a certain thing and with how many pins. The recorded information would then be brought home and entered into the computer along with the many stories I was told. I'd do the same thing after someone sent me an e-mail or stopped me on the street to tell me how they hung out their wash.

One Sunday in early February 2003 while I was listening to *The Vinyl Café* with Stuart McLean on CBC my radio transmission turned into static. I wrote Stuart and told him what had happened. I asked if he would be interested in mentioning my project on the show. This would be a wonderful way to reach people across the nation. Stuart replied he'd be "delighted" to mention my project. He asked where I lived and said I could return the favour by going clothesline hunting with him, giving him something to write about while taping some shows in Nova Scotia. Needless to say, I could not turn down such a wonderful offer.

We met in Wolfville on a lovely Sunday morning, drove around the Annapolis Valley and checked out quite a few lines. Stuart opened his shows in Wolfville and Halifax talking about our adventure. It was an incredible launch for the project. E-mails, letters, and phone calls started to pour in. Everyone was so enthusiastic and Stuart really set in motion my commitment to see this through to the end.

Soon afterwards, Carla Adams contacted me to do a segment for CBC Radio's *Maritime Noon*, which then went to national syndication, resulting in more mail. In September of 2003, Bill Spurr wrote a full-page article in the *Sunday Chronicle Herald* – more mail started to arrive.

In the summer of 2004, Janet Smith, then producer of CBC-TV's *On the Road Again* with Wayne Rostad, contacted me. We spent three days together filming a segment for the show. It was a great deal of fun. More and more mail. In October of 2005, Patty Mintz wrote an article in *The Regional*, a collective of local papers in the Annapolis Valley.

This exposure provided me with a vast amount of information to formulate my book. The experience of meeting people and listening to what they had to say about such a simple item has been illuminating and very entertaining.

This may be a good time to mention my own line. From a very young child, I have been fascinated by the patience, determination and pride people have taken in creating such fine lines. Watching the clothesline genre through my own family has instilled a part of tradition I am ever so thankful for having. Since starting this project, I have to admit, I have tried many varied ways of hanging the same item. One day I had five T-shirts on the line, all hung differently. While not aesthetically pleasing, from a research point of view it proved most beneficial.

I met a woman who believed if she didn't hang her clothes out the same way every time something bad would happen. Obsessive/compulsive behaviour? Maybe, maybe not. Old habits die hard and even though I know hanging something differently may actually improve the drying time and the wrinkle resistance, I continue to put clothes on the line the way I have for years. On occasion, I will break from tradition and go against the status quo, exert my rebelliousness and birthright.

The key to all of this is that there is no absolute right or wrong way to hang your laundry. Clotheslines are all over the world. They are a cultural phenomenon. Wherever you travel, you will eventually come across a clothesline. Each will reflect a characteristic of an area, a people, a life. This book is my reflection.

Sit back, relax and with common sense and good humour, read this book. In the process, I am sure you will recall your own memorable clothesline moments.

1

Drying Days

Drying days are naturally very important. Have you ever heard someone say, "What a great drying day"? Growing up, I had a sense this meant something quite important, but I didn't know for sure what it was. I did know that good drying days were sunny, warm and breezy, but I didn't fully understand the importance of the combination.

Traditionally, Mondays were laundry days. Lines would be full on a Monday morning, weather permitting. Over time, this extended to include Thursdays. Then, Saturday joined the team. Today, this trio remains the people's choice.

Following traditional lines (OK, I couldn't resist), Sunday was considered a day of rest and you did not do laundry. If for some reason you had to wash clothes, "by God, they best be off the line before church takes in."

With lifestyles changing, you find traditions changing too. Clotheslines have not been exempt. Now you can hang your laundry any day you want, weather permitting. This is totally acceptable and strongly encouraged.

Speaking of the weather, the key components in determining ideal drying conditions are wind, sun, temperature and humidity. Most will agree, the best drying days are those with a medium breeze (twenty-five kilometres or fifteen miles an hour), warm temperatures (ranging between 10° to 25°C, 50° to 80°F), sunny, and no humidity.

Of course, these conditions are not always waiting for us when we arrive at the stoop. When conditions are right and the laundry is on the line, you feel harmonious with nature. On the other hand, when conditions are less than ideal, you may ponder the results of your labour and consider strike action.

In ideal conditions, clothes of heavy or medium weight will dry in three hours. Variances in weather conditions impact drying time. Common sense? To many of us yes, but remember, not everyone has common sense. More importantly, it is our responsibility to teach the fine art of clothesline use, right down to the last detail.

In the event your clothes succumb to wet weather, it is advisable to bring them in, run them through the spin cycle, and rehang when conditions improve. Remember, very wet laundry makes for a stressed line. If you continuously allow your line to undergo heavy strain, it will break, much like us. Treat your line right and it will treat you right.

Tip: Hint passed down from my grandmother: hang a heavy sock as the last item on the line (closest to you). When the sock is dry, you will know everything else on the line is dry too.

In spring and fall, it is a good plan to have the clothes on the line by mid-morning (9 a.m.) and off the line by mid-afternoon (3 p.m.), if not sooner. Otherwise, the clothes will start to get damp, thus defeating the entire purpose. Of course, it is critical to have the laundry off the line "before the stories come on TV." With the introduction of cable television and VCRs, I don't know if this is as important as it used to be.

Some of us hang the laundry out at night, seemingly to appear ahead of the game. After all, having the laundry washed and out before 7 a.m. is quite impressive. Late night hanging typically requires a light, which in turn attracts mosquitoes. Hanging in the dark is of course an option. A squeaky line may jeopardize this plan.

When conditions are good, I have found you can get two, maybe three lines of laundry dried in a day.

Think of the savings on your power bill. One woman told me her record for the most number of loads for one day (washed and completely air-dried outside) was seven! Of course, you cannot leave your place of employment to load and unload the line, but if you have another person at home, let's say between the ages of ten and twenty, chances are they have very good hand-eye coordination, a skill attained from the use of various electronic gadgetry. I am sure they could very quickly learn the operation of clothespin placement and removal. Trainees are not restricted by age or gender and no formal training is required. Pay is negotiable. May I suggest the amount you save on electricity.

Tip: Some people like to bring cotton items off the line when they are slightly damp because it makes ironing easier. If you can persuade your trainee to iron, consider yourself a lottery winner!

During summer months, the significance of time on the line is not as important simply because weather conditions are typically better. If the humidity is high, drying time will be considerably longer. One load may take as long as six hours to dry, especially if there is no wind.

Tip: Need to mow the lawn? Avoid grass clippings from sticking to your laundry by mowing before *the clothes are hung or* after *they're removed from the line.*

In winter, drying conditions present much more of a challenge. Anyone who has hung laundry on the line in the cold likely relates more to the amount of time it takes to regain the feeling in your fingers than the amount of time it takes to dry the clothes. Sunshine and a brisk breeze are more important in the winter. No point hanging clothes out at night; as soon as the sun comes up is best.

If temperatures are below the freezing mark, you may want to reconsider. Frozen clothes need to be freed from the line much the same way you pry frozen pork chops apart. Frozen sheets tend to take on the same properties as plywood. The larger the frozen item, the more space required to thaw it. Your house can suddenly be transformed into a giant paper doll cut-out clothing factory. It is not recommended to fold frozen laundry. On very cold days, you may not even get the clothes out of the basket before they freeze into one solid form.

Tip: Leaving clothes on the line through a frost or through dense fog will help brighten your whites. Years ago, people placed their linens over bushes or on the ground to take advantage of this whitening process. Bright sunshine can have the same effect.

It goes without saying, rainy days are good for the garden, not for the clothesline. In smog-free areas, rain provides an extra rinse. Some claim this hardens the clothes, others say it softens them. In smoggy areas, you will need to rewash the clothes if they have been soaked.

This brings us to the question of how long you leave a line of laundry on the line. On and off the line the same day is ideal. Leaving clothes on the line for twenty-four to thirty-six hours is acceptable. Longer is not. They start to lose their lustre and begin to fade. I heard a story about someone who left a comforter on the line too long and it began to disintegrate. It wasn't from the weather; it was from a squirrel who decided to use it for nesting material. Another person told me a similar story, except it was a shirt and the birds were using it for new home construction. From what I can deduce, nature's statute of limitations amounts to three days. After that, the gloves are off, maybe literally.

I met a woman who claimed to hold the record for having clothes on the line for the longest amount of time . . . seven days. Her line started to take on the properties of her closet: whenever she wanted anything, she just went to the line and got it. No records related to clotheslines seem to exist. There is no record of the longest, the oldest, the strongest – nothing. The market is wide open. I will admit, I have seen camper lines with a cup towel hanging on them in the fall and the same cup towel is still there the following spring. Of course, this is likely more of an oversight than an intentional act.

Generally, clothes are not left on the line overnight. Some diehard enthusiasts will bring them in even if they are not dry and hang them out again the next day, weather permitting. Why? Apparently, at one time it was believed, if you left your laundry on the line overnight, you would be considered lazy or disorderly. I wouldn't touch that with a ten-foot prop.

This story was told to me by a man living in the Bahamas. He said when their house was being built, his mom asked for a roof over the back porch. "Why?" asked his dad. "So I can hang clothes out if it is raining," she replied. "Why would you want to hang clothes out in the rain?" he countered. The porch never got a roof.

Whether you decide to leave your clothes on the line overnight or in the rain, the decision is yours to make. As a wise man once told me, put the clothes on the line when they are wet and take the clothes off the line when they're dry.

2

Clothesline Styles

Driving through the countryside, you will undoubt-edly pass many different types of clotheslines. Some communities favour one over another. Essentially, there are five different types. We have the Basic (Camper Line), the Prop, the Stationary, the Pulley, and the Umbrella (Dryer Line).

Basic Line: I like to refer to this line also as the camper line because it is traditionally the type found around camps and cottages. It is very simple. Camper lines are strung between two stationary objects about eye level. Because of this, it is very important that persons other than you also know its location. This

The Basic Line

is especially important should you be moving at high speed. I recommend you hang something, anything, on the line at all times.

Prop Line: This line is just the same as the basic line, except it uses a prop. A prop is a skinny pole used to raise and brace the line against the wind. Typically, a prop line is longer than the basic line. The prop is usually made of wood with a notch in the top for the line to rest. Some people prefer a hole drilled through the prop and the line strung through, thus eliminating the chance of the prop becoming disengaged.

I was in the car one day listening to the radio when I heard an elderly gentleman call in to a talk show and speak about a childhood memory. He told

DOUG VAN HEMESSEN PHOTO

of a man he knew who travelled about his small outport home in Newfoundland selling "spears" to the local people for their clotheslines. I smiled and laughed. What a wonderful memory and even better that he called in to share it with us all.

Personally, I find prop lines the most picturesque. Before starting this book, I only had a basic line and a pulley line, but now I have all three. It is tricky to get used to incorporating the prop when you first begin because you have to learn to move it higher as you hang more things on the line. Over time, I have gotten much better.

The Stationary Line: The stationary line, if you have ever seen a line of this kind hung in the manner in which it was designed, is truly a beautiful sight. Understanding its design simply enhances your appreciation. You will find this line as visually pleasing as the prop line and with the added uniformity it strikes you as having achieved the ultimate.

The stationary line is a favourite and you don't see many of them anymore. Construction and maintenance are more involved, plus you may need to shovel a path to get to them in the winter. This line has two posts about fifteen to thirty feet (five to ten metres) apart. Each post has a cross member with two to four parallel lines strung between them. Each line serves a significant purpose. The outer lines house the linens, providing privacy for the inner lines which hold your more intimate apparel. Meaningful, practical, and perfect. Some people like to adorn their main masts with bird houses or flags. This simply adds to the charm.

Tip: Birdhouses encourage birds . . . birds poop . . . a lot. You may want to face the bird house door away from the actual line.

The Pulley Line: I can attest to the fact the pulley line is the easiest to use. By easiest, I mean the time and physical energy you need to expend is much less than the other designs. However, the other designs may provide more satisfaction because of the added labour. You can figure that one out on your own and let me know.

The pulley line is by far the most common and popular line of today. It is more complicated in regard to installation and requires some maintenance, but the ease of operation outweighs any installation woes . . . to the hanging operator, anyway.

Your pulley line is strung between two supports, each able to house a large hook which has a pulley placed on it. The line is strung through the pulleys and joined with — you got it — a joiner.

The length can vary as well as the type and size of pulley. It is strongly recommended you use metal pulleys, the average size being 6.5 inches (16.5 centimetres) in diameter. I need to point out, it is important to consider the amount of laundry you intend to regularly put on the line and the average wind conditions in your yard. It is recommended you not exceed seventy-five feet (twenty-three metres). Arriving home to discover your clothes lying on the ground is a situation where innocent onlookers may be at risk of serious personal injury. Understand, it is a most disheartening sight.

The disadvantage of the pulley line is that you cannot easily retrieve a certain item. Should you want your yellow shirt, you may need to remove a number of items in order to reach it.

The Umbrella Line (Dryer Line): You have likely spotted these lines neatly tucked in someone's backyard. Most people I have interviewed do not prefer this style. That is not to say this line should be abandoned. You, eleven people, who proudly stated your preference should be commended for defending your position among the masses. The umbrella is often used in conjunction with another type of line.

These lines, or dryers as most hardware outlets call them, are more contemporary and convenient backyard urban space savers. You may have already discovered areas where the only option to hang clothes outside is to use an umbrella line. They come in various shapes and sizes; some rotate and some don't. Some have concentric lines and others have parallel lines. Friends told me about a particular Aussie model they saw at a home show in British Columbia. They were so taken with it, they contacted the Australian consulate, who located the maker and the distributor. They were impressed with the sturdiness and the size. Generally speaking, though, umbrellas are limiting simply due to the design. Whether square or triangular in shape, if your umbrella has concentric lines the outside perimeter provides the greatest amount of hanging space. Each concentric inner line shortens in length, restricting the size of items which can be hung on it. By design, the umbrella line compels you to arrange your laundry according to size.

One gentleman told me about an umbrella line where the owner greased the ball bearings and when the wind picked up, it spun so fast it looked like a propeller.

Tip: Before investing or erecting any clothesline, check with your local by-laws to insure it is legally permissible. Some areas, urban and rural, will not permit clotheslines of any design. If you are asking yourself why they are banned in certain areas, it is because they are considered unsightly. You heard it – unsightly – not a fire hazard or any other such viable excuse. They are considered distasteful and that's that.

Listen to this story from a woman who was about to sign on the dotted line.

"After my husband and I married we were negotiating to buy a house . . . Things were going along very well until at the last minute they presented us with a document to sign to the effect that we would not keep a used car lot or auto body shop *or clothesline* on our property. Well! I was insulted! Refused to sign and bought a house elsewhere. The real estate agent couldn't believe my attitude and my husband was not too pleased at the time, but after thirty years together he is just as glad, as he reaps the benefit of the heavenly fresh laundry."

And another: "When I was a student at the Alberta College of Art and Design . . . one project I did was to construct a clothesline on the premises of the school, which just happened to be next to the Jubilee Auditorium. I thought it was great to have a clothesline, which is forbidden in many parts of the city, to be next to the concert hall. I am not convinced the teacher was as impressed."

Before we move on, I have to tell you about a patented pin-less clothesline. At the Redcliff Museum, in Redcliff, Alberta, on display is a pin-less clothesline patented and manufactured by the Redcliff Specialty Company in 1910-1915. An article in the *Redcliff Review* boasted about how this wonderful new clothesline eliminated the need for any more clothespins. An excerpt reads: "The clothesline is made of the best of wire and is so constructed that the bother and expense of the old-fashioned clothes pin is done away with. It is made up of a series of loops an equal distance apart so arranged that the articles to be hung up, no matter what size, are held securely. Scores of these lines are already on the market and are giving entire satisfaction."

While the concept was clever, the practicality lends itself to many problems. I am not sure how tightly the loops grasped each item, but manipulation of each loop would be difficult, especially if it were cold. Too, I cannot see how your clothes would be free of pinch marks. In order to hang a full load of wash you would need a considerable number of links. I suspect the cost of the wire would be greater than the cost of replacing pins. I can honestly say, I have never used one, nor heard of anyone else using one, so my views are simply speculative. Honestly, though, I believe part of the charm of hanging clothes is well-balanced pinning.

Of course, you could always gather together some friends and stand about, each holding onto the end of an article until it is dried. Don't laugh – this practice was often done in India by women washing their silk wares in the Ganges River. It likely made for good conversation and strong bodies.

The Other Line: The "other line" is the line hidden behind your main line. You could refer to it as the "line of temptation." This line is ingeniously strung to mask its presence. You'll often find intimate apparel, stained items, torn items or cleaning cloths on this line. It is meant to hold those items you'd like to keep private.

The hanging rack.

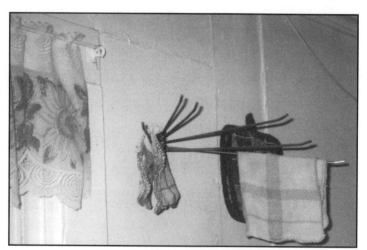

This swing-away rack hangs on a wall.

Inside Lines

I want to quickly refer to the inside lines, of which there are four.

The Hanging Rack: The simplest and easiest to install. This can be either a single pole or a combination of poles hooked together. It is hung over a heat source, traditionally the kitchen wood stove. Some of the more elaborate racks have a pulley system which allows you to raise and lower the rack. Open-ended racks are ideal for drying mittens.

The Swing-Away Rack: This cleverly designed rack is cheap, functional and easy to use. Mount this rack wherever you need a place to dry small, regularly wet items. When not in use, it can easily be folded away. Traditionally, these racks were found near a sink, inside a cupboard, on a wall near a heat source or near a window.

Tip: When locating a rack near a heat source, make sure the placement is at a safe distance to avoid any risk of fire. You want your items dried, not burned.

The Collapsible Rack: This rack is commonly used today as a "laundry room assistant." It serves much the same function as the swing-away with the added bonus of mobility. You can accommodate a number of items at one time and when it is not needed, collapse it and store it away.

The Full-Sized Upright Folding Rack: This is the very first clothing drying apparatus I can recall seeing in my house as a child. We had a rack of this type which we kept in the basement near the wood furnace. At the time, electric dryers were not common household appliances, so the rainy day dryer was the rack. It unfolded much like a formal letter standing on its edge. Generally, it would be a three- or four-fold (brace) rack standing approximately six feet tall with four rungs on each fold (brace). Because these racks were larger, they were able to hold more than the aforementioned racks.

You've heard the importance of the phrase "location, location, location." Obviously, you can see where the same applies to the placement of your racks. Many variables have to be taken into account. You have to consider the dimensions of the room, the traffic flow in the room, the drying conditions of the provided space as well as the practicality of the location. Attics were seldom used because they were too cold in the winter, too hot in the summer and simply too difficult to access with heavy baskets of laundry. Unused rooms or dry basements were common spaces. Many had a heat source which quickened the drying time.

You can appreciate why laundry was such an important chore to have started early in the morning – it was very time-consuming. First off, you had to gather and sort the laundry. Then wash the clothes (often by hand using a washboard or via the infamous wringer washer). Finally, came the drying process. As one load dried, another would be waiting to take its place. Naturally, keeping the house warm was important, which meant feeding the fire regularly (I wouldn't be a bit surprised if there was bread in the oven, too). Of course, the more people in your household, the more laundry you had and the more space you needed to dry it. Children often found the racks a delightful play area. Any rambunctious play activity would result in a strict calling which you quickly learned. It started with your full birth name followed by "get away from there or else!"

3

Clothesline Underpinnings

There are a few things we must discuss which pertain to the operation of the clothesline. Some have changed over time but many have stayed the same. These things are the components needed to safely get the laundry on and off the line.

Where and How

Where you are going to put your clothesline is crucial. The most important things to consider are safety and convenience. Be wary of crossing driveways, other people's property (which means asking if you can mount your clothesline apparatus on their tree), walkways, pools, or stretches where heavy equipment may need to pass through. For example, if you have oil delivery, water delivery, snow plows, or farm equipment crossing your property, don't string a line in their way. Naturally, there is always one over-zealous operator in the pack who will find your line and knock it out of commission . . . you know who you are. Power lines are not a problem unless you are considering an upper level line, such as in an apartment. Always lean on the side of caution whenever you are dealing with power lines and contact your local power company if you have any doubts about safety.

If you are planning to use a tree as one or both of your posts, make sure it is a mature tree. If you mount a pulley on a young tree, it will virtually grow around the pulley, rendering it useless. You tell me softwood trees can be sappy and harbour more bugs than hardwood trees. If your only option is a softwood tree, some clever people devise an extension, which allows the functional pulley to extend away from the tree, keeping the laundry out of harm's way.

Your line should be placed where it catches the breeze and is able to take advantage of the longest period of exposed sunlight. Typically, an eastern or southerly exposure is best. Stand in your yard at sunrise and at the first glimpse of the sun, watch the path it crosses. This will help determine the direction your line should be facing.

For convenience and privacy, most clotheslines are located just outside the back door. Some are connected to the house and others are free standing. The exit closest to the laundry room is really convenient, unless of course that would mean your clothesline crosses the front yard. While I know many of you are frowning at this possibility, front yard lines are becoming more familiar. I guess for some of you, wherever the tree is, the clothesline is. Works for me.

Some areas in Scotland had specific poles designed for communal use. In addition to your clothes basket, you would carry your line – rope in most cases. After drying and removing your laundry, you would take down your rope, freeing the pole for the next person. Rope was hard to come by and could be very expensive, and no one dared risk it being stolen.

In Singapore, it is common to see bamboo poles (usually four) on the balconies of high-rise apartments. Apparently, in Singapore people would say they have "a one-pole wash" or a "four-pole wash."

Now of course comes the question of length. Longer is not necessarily better. Excess length can be a problem. It would be better if you frequented the line more often. I find you can get two loads of laundry on a fifty- to sixty-foot (fifteen- to eighteen-metre) line.

Clothepins

DOUG VAN HEMESSEN PHOTO

Pins are essential tools. Selecting clothespins may seem to be a simple enough task, but if you are truly devoted you will understand the vital importance of quality pins. You want your pins to be durable, smooth and clean, and you want a lot of them. One day I saw a sheet pinned to a line with over twenty-two pins on it! I couldn't count anymore because my eyes kept crossing. There must have been over two hundred pins on that one line. It looked like an army of soldiers standing abreast just waiting to march into battle. Now that I think of it, I have a clothespin Christmas tree ornament designed to look like a soldier. Actually, it is a clothespeg. Speaking of pegs, if you are fortunate enough to have the older style pegs, value them highly. I am told the newer styles are shorter and do not grasp and hold items as well as their senior counterparts.

The vast majority of us use wooden pins. A good wood pin will be made of softwood and have a strong, tight, good working metal spring. Most are between three to four inches long (five to eight centimetres).

When faced with having to replace pins, make sure you examine the quality closely. Poorly made pins are generally cut wrong or have the spring placed too close to the bottom, which doesn't allow for a good grip. Some pins are too short or too light-weight.

One woman told me the life span of a wooden pin to be approximately a year and a half if you leave them exposed to the weather year round. When I asked how she knew this, she said by the remains of pins gone by, now resting peacefully (or should I say piecefully) at the base of her umbrella line.

Plastic pins, of various colours, are also available. I have found plastic pins to be less durable. They tend to break more easily and develop rough edges. On the other hand, I know people who would have nothing else. Whatever your personal preference, take care of your pins . . . after all, they *are* holding your clothes up.

I met a woman who colour coordinated her laundry with her pins. For instance, blue pins for blue items, red for red, and so on. It made for a stunning line.

Tip: Before using new pins (wooden ones), try soaking them in water overnight. I am told this softens them and makes them more weather tolerant.

I will not delve too much into pin containers, as the list is vast. Here is the short list: flower pots, ice cream containers, buckets, Easter baskets, onion bags, old roasters, and aprons. When my children were smaller, they took the clothespins, dumped them onto the floor and made "trains" by hooking the pins together.

Have you ever been to a baby shower and played the clothespin game? The point of this game is to see how many pins you can hold in one hand without dropping any. To play, hold a clotheshanger with about twenty pins on it in one hand and using the other hand try to remove as many pins as you can without dropping any. You are not allowed to use the hanger or your body to shore up the pins you are trying to hold on to.

At your child's next birthday party you might want to play a very simple clothespin game. All you need are clothespins and a milk bottle. Since you are not apt to have a milk bottle, any narrow-necked bottle big enough for the pins to fall through will suffice. To play, stand over the bottle and see how many pins you can drop inside.

Baskets

Your basket is a key piece of equipment. As many of you have expressed, there is a direct correlation between the placement of clothes into the basket and the end result on the line. A basket may look like a simple tool, but it carries a great deal of responsibility.

As one gentleman told me, "Gradually, I found myself taking the clothes out of the washer and putting the smaller items such as face cloths, socks, undies, in the bottom of the basket and working my way up to the larger items such as jeans, towels, sweaters, so I could organize my clothesline by size starting with the biggest items."

I know many of you are nodding your head right now.

Baskets vary in make and model. I have to admit, there is something unique about an old wicker basket, perhaps because it holds more memories. One of my very first recollections is of sitting in a wicker basket. I must have been very young. I can't recall whose basket it was, but it seems to have made a lasting impression. Now that I think of it, my children slept in a wicker basket when they were infants.

Rectangular, plastic baskets are the most popular, followed by square, then oval and finally round. Ergonomic baskets (kidney-shaped) are not very common, though my son uses his faithfully. Many people still use oval wicker baskets. Most say the older styles are best because they are stronger and smoother. You might say, they are aged to perfection.

Bring your basket in between loads to prevent it from blowing away or getting wet. Children like to get inside baskets and be pulled around the yard. Dogs like to chew them and cats like to sleep in them. A lot of people like to use their baskets to carry in the groceries. I use an old basket with a torn handle to store all my gift-wrapping paraphernalia. My basket served me faithfully for years and when it became disabled, I felt obliged to find it another very important and valuable job.

Line Devices

Over the years the clothesline has had its share of technological advances. We now have what is referred to as an elevator. This device eliminates the need for a stoop, which in itself requires upkeep in order to maintain a safe work area. The elevator is mounted on a secure building or pole at the beginning of the line. When you lower the elevator, your line is easily accessible and once the laundry is in order and pushed out into the desired drying area, it is simply

A clothesline pulley attached to an elevator.

a matter of pulling the cord and raising the elevator to the desired height.

Other devices you can find at the local hardware store include various sized pulleys, fasteners, joiners, spacers or dividers and of course, line.

Let's quickly examine each of these, starting with the most important.

Clothesline: Typical line is plastic-coated steel cable. It is durable and easy to work with. It is sold in fifty-foot (fifteen-metre) coils in four main colours: blue, green, yellow or clear. Maybe the colour choice is a designer feature – yellow house with a yellow line.

Line is sold according to strength, ranging from 500-pound test, 1,000-pound test and 1,350-pound test. To determine the strength you will need, ask yourself a few simple questions:

1. Is my line long?
2. Is it windy where I live?
3. Do I often use my line?
4. Do I hang out full loads of laundry?
5. Have I ever witnessed or experienced a downed line?

If you can answer yes to one of these questions, seriously consider quality when shopping.

Prior to plastic-coated cables, people wrapped white cotton strips around their line to insure cleanliness. Some people placed wax paper over their line before hanging any finery.

I understand it is still possible to purchase stainless steel cable with no coating which is very durable and ranges in price. One gentleman told me he installed a line of this type in 1967 "and it is as good today as it was then." Some people like to use braided wire for clothesline. As the aforementioned gentleman said (and I agree), "The only thing you *must* do is clean it with a good solvent to remove any oil that is on it from the manufacturing process." Other people prefer to use galvanized cable (840-pound working load).

One gentleman told me about a neighbour of his who always took his line down if a lightning storm was pending. I have not heard of lightning travelling

DOUG VAN HEMESSEN PHOTO

along a clothesline, but I have heard of it travelling along power or telephone lines.

Pulleys: You will need to determine the size and number of pulleys you want in order to know how much line to purchase. Metal pulleys are recommended for outdoor use. They can range in size from 5¹/₂ to 8 inches (14 to 20 centimetres). Some people tell me they prefer the four pulley system because it helps prevent the laundry from blowing and twisting over the upper line. For that reason, some people use a bicycle wheel. Before you invest, I would suggest you ask the same questions as above, and buy quality.

Joiner: This is an important device as it literally holds your line together. Joiners also act as tighteners. They are reasonably cheap and worth every cent. You can purchase clips to prevent the ends from fraying.

Another device is a *spacer or divider,* also referred to as a spreader. This simple item is designed specifically for pulley lines which tend to sag deeply when housing a full load of laundry, or for lines holding heavier things. Simply clip it over the upper line and then under the bottom line when you begin to notice a gap developing which is wider than the normal width of the line. Should you choose to ignore this developing problem, you run the risk of your clothes dragging on the ground or your line breaking, regardless of weather conditions. This tool, which you may

A spacer, divider or spreader.

Spacers at work.

use more than one of, helps to eliminate stress points by maintaining an even line spread.

Some spacers have metal pulleys or grooves to hold them in place. On occasion, spacers become disengaged and caught in the item next to it. Generally, this does not pose a significant inconvenience because you will be able to gently shake the line and cause the divider to fall freely to the ground. Yanking on the line in an attempt to wilfully remount the spacer is pointless.

I was actually quite surprised to discover clothesline kits exist. A great idea. A kit usually consists of line, two pulleys, a joiner, and a spacer/spreader/divider. As a matter of fact, the same gentleman who told me about his stainless steel line also suggested giving a clothesline as a wedding gift. I think it is a wonderful idea!

Maintenance

With regards to maintenance, the best bit of advice is to keep your pins and basket clean and dry. Periodically check any moveable parts and replace any worn or frayed line. Proper maintenance will insure the line sustains mechanical dependability.

Tip: Always be on the alert for new and improved gadgetry.

Owning a good, sturdy ladder is considered an important tool for the clothesline.

4

On the Line

Two controversial issues exist about clotheslines – the order in which you hang your clothes out and how you hang each item. Since starting this project, I have learned (as you are about to) the many and varied ways of hanging a single item on the line, not to mention in conjunction with all the other items on the line.

During my research, I travelled about with a basket of clothes, a notepad, a pen, and a camera. The same basket, containing the same items, was used for each interview. I would hold up each article and ask each interviewee how they would hang it on the line. One person would say "this way," another would say "that way," and another, rather quietly, might indicate yet another way.

I always laughed when individuals responded to a technique other than their own. "You do?!" "You do not!?" Or "What?!" Or, "Yes, they do it that way, I've seen their lines." All common responses. Some people simply nodded "yes" or "no" when asked as to how they hung a particular item. If they nodded "no" to all the ways I thought possible, I would have to ask them to demonstrate. People were very cooperative and proud to display their own style. Some were rather shocked to discover not everyone did it their way, especially when it came to undergarments.

One particular woman had a method of hanging her underwear which was so intricate it defied the methodology of "ease of operation." I am about to share with you the various techniques and methods for hanging clothes on the line. Remember . . . what you are about to read is the truth.

Hanging Techniques

The placement of articles on the line is somewhat debatable in itself. Whether you decide the first thing on the line should be the largest, the smallest, the lightest, the darkest, the heaviest or the last thing out of the washer is based upon a few factors.

Regardless of which school of thought you were taught or developed on your own, how you hang your clothes out depends upon the type of line you have and its location. The geography of your yard and its free-standing structures, along with the degree of activity the line may encounter, can be key elements to the placement of your clothes.

Traditionally, the *white wash* was always done first because each consecutive load caused the wash water to get dirtier. Hence, the white/cleanest load was first and the dark/dirtiest load was last. This is still very common.

Often, a *linen wash* was done and hung out by itself. A linen wash would consist of sheets, pillow cases, towels, wash cloths, cup towels, dish cloths or any other such articles. Your line of regular clothes would follow. Undergarments were not washed with kitchen linens. You can still find linen lines and they are very pretty to look at; the colour of the different sized rectangles blowing in the wind or simply hanging still is very picturesque.

Today, with the introduction of germ-killing detergents, along with the pressure to conserve energy and water, and the time you have allotted to doing laundry, this practice has fallen to the wayside. About a quarter of the people I interviewed wash kitchen linens separately, often washing by hand with bleach to insure their cleanliness.

Throughout my interviews I discovered the majority of people use a pulley clothesline. For that reason, I am going to tell you how most people choose to hang their laundry on the pulley line. Like I said, most of you continue to choose to hang your white load first, starting with the largest item, usually bedding, followed by towels, and gradually working your way along decreasing lengths, ending up with your underwear or socks being the last item on the line.

Others of you choose to do just the opposite, starting with your underwear or socks and working towards having the largest items being the last item on the line. You tell me you do it this way because your sheets usually dry quicker; therefore, you can remove them to free up more line space for your next load.

Either way you choose, or either colour you decide to start with, your clothes form a wedge on the line. When you add the next load of laundry you tend to follow the same pattern, so you either form two similar wedges or two facing wedges.

Some people prefer to hang their dark load first. Generally speaking, this line usually takes the longest time to dry because it would include work pants and jeans, for example. Naturally, the white wash would follow.

If you are a real devotee of the clothesline, sorting by colour and size can go to another level. Try hanging each colour by its single hue. Listen to this: "For example, each blue garment is exactly the same shade of blue, as are the pink, green and yellow. Sizes are carefully hung from smallest to largest, colours are never mixed and even in the foulest cold weather the clothes are out flapping in the breeze. Awesome!"

Some of you use the same principle when you decide to hang the heaviest items out first, continuing along with your lightest weight items being last. Your heavy to light line will not generally follow a size methodology, but rather take a more utilitarian

approach. Some of you like to hang by colour, but the majority of utilitarians mix the colours and concentrate strictly on the weight of the item, knowing your heaviest items need the longest time on the line in order to dry; hence they are first on and last off. Your focus is completely logical and your concern lies completely with the drying of the clothes.

Regardless of the items being hung out to dry, the consistency rule was evident. For instance, some people like to hang everything over the line about five to ten centimetres (two to four inches) or else you hang everything upside down, or inside out or by the seams. Everyone has a comfort level and seldom strays from it, even haphazard people.

If your line is not parallel to the ground, but instead has one end higher or lower than the other, the tendency would be to hang the larger items out first. For example: if one pulley is attached to the side of your house and the other pulley is thirty feet up a spruce tree, chances are you will want to hang your sheets out first. On the other hand, if the pulley attached to your house is higher, you may want to hang the sheets out last. This provides for freer movement and lessens the chance of them dragging on the ground or being caught by something travelling under your line. Naturally, your line should be at least six feet off the ground, regardless of which end we are talking about.

Obstacles such as shrubs or trees, deck rails, dog houses, pools, and so on, along the path of your clothesline, may require you to hang your clothes in a pattern to fit between these items. You will find developing this pattern to be time-consuming and possibly nerve-wracking, but you can do it. One might suggest moving the line to a more suitable location if possible or relocating some of the obstacles.

Another factor to consider when you hang out your clothes is the length of your line. If you are fortunate enough to have a long line, you likely don't need to be concerned about having to remove items to allow for other pieces. Some of you with shorter lines often do a white wash one day and a dark wash another day.

Should you be using a prop line, the larger items, regardless of colour, are placed nearest to the prop. Often, the white wash would be on one side of the

DOUG VAN HEMESSEN PHOTO

prop and the dark wash on the other side. This makes for a very aesthetically pleasing line. If you use more than one prop, chances are they are of varying lengths. Longer props allow larger/heavier things to be placed in between and raised further off the ground.

Should you be using an umbrella line, the smaller items are on the inside, with each tier gradually housing larger items, with sheets being on the outside. The umbrella line leaves a person little choice in choosing where to place items on the line. It is predetermined by the structure of the unit itself; shorter lines are closer to the centre pole, larger spaces for larger items border the outside. You still find most people choosing to hang a full white or dark wash on the umbrella, as opposed to a mixture of colours. Whether you use the colour rule or the weight rule, either works equally well on an umbrella.

As I travelled about, it is remarkable the number of places you find a clothesline. Places you wouldn't necessarily expect to see one. Take the ferry from Nova Scotia to Newfoundland and Labrador, you might find a retractable clothesline in the shower of the cabin. A retractable three-string line, perfect. Hotels often have similar types.

I have had people tell me how much they love their clothesline. One woman informed me, "When my husband proposed to me I told him yes, but I had to have a clothesline before our wedding day. A few days before, I told him I was serious and he got busy and put one up for me!"

Many people report how unhappy they are when they need to move and leave their clothesline only to discover that clotheslines are not allowed in the new location. I have heard such stories from many of the seniors I have had the pleasure of meeting. Some had to leave their home and move into a complex, which sounds rigid enough as it is, but when they told me about having to leave their clothesline behind, you could actually see and feel their loss and disappointment. When I asked if they were allowed to have a clothesline where they were living, some said they could share a line, and others said they were not allowed. "Oh well, I'm likely too old to carry the basket any way. The girls are good here; they do my laundry for me."

One woman wrote me and said, "In some of the upscale subdivisions here in Ontario clotheslines are banned! Can you believe it? I always say I would like to see anyone tell *me* I can't hang my clothes out!"

Another woman wrote, "I am 60 now, and still think of my mother when I hang out clothes, it is a good memory."

You and I both know, what makes or breaks a fine line is its orderly fashion: the placement of each item is very important to the overall appearance.

One woman I interviewed told me: "I was living next to Jill for about three years when one day she sighed and said, 'I have been trying not to say anything, but do you know that you hang your clothes all wrong?' I did not, as a matter of fact, know this, nor had I any idea that there could be a right and wrong for such a thing. The one rule I did follow was to hang my underwear close to the house and yes, if possible, behind the towels. Jill pointed out to me how much more pleasing it was to hang all the pants together, then all the shirts, then towels, small items, and of course underwear at the end so that they hung near the house. Dresses, skirts, etc. hung, if possible, on a separate line. Sheets hung on a line alone. I did laugh at her, but once I started doing it this way, I have since been bothered by the clothes-lines of others."

Doesn't that just about say it all?

If you compare a line where time was taken to insure things were consistently hung evenly and straight to one more randomly hung, with no established pattern or unity, it becomes clear where the harmony rests.

As one woman told me she learned from her mother about the importance of orderly fashion: "You wouldn't want Mrs. Jones up the road or Mrs. Smith down the road to drive by, see the clothes on the line and not hanging right. They would know, for sure, that your house must look the same, messy and untidy." She told me she has hung things on the line, turned around to look at it and thought, "My mother would not be happy with the way that looks" and would promptly pull it in and rearrange it.

A retired police officer told me he began taking on the task of doing the laundry and hanging it out when his wife went away for the weekend. He admitted not having any specific technique when he started: "It was total chaos." He quickly learned to organize his basket, then to strategically put them on the line: "I just can't put clothes on the line any-more, without almost measuring the length of each item. I am almost at that stage of colour coordinating them so they don't look too contrasting, with the lake and the trees in the background. I hang them up and

Consistency and harmony

Total chaos.

then I walk down to the other end of the yard to see how they look on the line."

Not surprisingly, this is very common and while amusing, the really funny thing is, many of us do exactly what this man does. We often don't admit it publicly because we don't want other people to think we may be dysfunctional.

Hanging Methods

Just when you thought you had it all figured out, I am going to tell you how and why other lines differ from your own. I should warn you, this is apt to cause some shock and amazement. I strongly urge you to be of an open mind and a strong heart.

While you may question some of the following methods, trust me when I say I have tested most of them and some are not as odd as you may think. Feel free to experiment on your own, even if it is secretly done, because what you discover may surprise you.

I recall one group agreeing to hang their pants by the waistband, and then commenting, "Have you seen how So-and-So does it? She always hangs them by the leg. I don't understand why she does that." "Really? I never noticed that before." "You look next time. She does, I just don't know why."

If you feel obligated to teach your children, spouse, or friends how to hang the laundry, consider using these methods, as they may be more trainable than you give them credit for. I had a woman write me and say she was trying to teach her husband to hang out the clothes, but whenever he did, the sight made her crazy: "He hangs things helter-skelter, a sock, a pair of boxers, a sheet, the second sock and then three more unmatched socks!" She claims he is "untrainable," but she shouldn't give up. Maybe he just hasn't developed a method he is comfortable with – or maybe he has!

After one particular interview I conducted, a gentleman came up to me and began to explain how he hangs clothes on the line. Partway through, his wife piped up and said, "How do you know so much about something you never do?"

One thing I learned, if you intentionally hang one item inside out, chances are you hang every item inside out, claiming it prevents fading and allows pockets to dry better. The key is consistency.

Now you must clear your mind of all preconceptions because we are about to start putting our laundry on the line, piece by piece. We are going to use the same basket of clothes I used when conducting my interviews. The presentation of items is as they were packed and removed from the basket, not necessarily presented in the order you might place them in your basket or on the line.

Tip: Remember, it saves considerable time if you sort your laundry as you remove it from the washer, placing it in the basket in the reverse order of how you want it to look on the line.

Before we delve any further into finding out how people hang their laundry on the line, I discovered there are two basic approaches: either you stretch items to their fullest or you loop.

Looping means pinning in a continuously repeating loop-like pattern. Loops need to be consistent, meaning the distance between the pins and the loop size between the pins is equal. Larger items will have many loops in order to retain the symmetry created by looping. Whatever loop size you choose, it is important to maintain uniformity along the entire line. Looping requires a great deal of pins.

Tip: It is important to snap each item before you put it on the line. This is done by firmly grasping each piece and giving it a quick, sharp shake, hard enough to create a "snap" sound. This shakes off any loose debris and reduces wrinkling. "Snapping" is also important prior to folding your laundry, for the same reasons.

On to the task at hand, the first item out of my basket which, by the way, was a large plastic rectangular container with a lid, not your typical laundry basket.

Double flat sheet (cotton/print): Most of you choose to hang the sheet by matching the top and bottom seams, stretched to the fullest and pinned with three

The loop method. (DOUG VAN HEMESSEN PHOTO)

The straight method. (DOUG VAN HEMESSEN PHOTO)

to four pins. Because of the print, some of you reversed the sheet to prevent fading. Some people like to fold the sheet in half and pin it to the line along the fold, eliminating pin marks on the hems. Few of you chose to actually place the sheet over the line, but some say it depends on how windy it is. This was a new one to me – staggering the sheet, pinning the upper right-hand corner to the line then the bottom, right-hand corner, followed by the upper left and lower left, allowing for more air movement between the two sides. About two-thirds of you preferred stretching to the fullest, and for you, looping was only an option if you were trying to conserve space on the line. Some of you claim sheets dry better if looped.

Fitted sheet (solid/flannel): The groans uttered and mumbles of "oh, those damn things!" told me I was holding the renegade of the basket. Most of you chose to hang this sheet by the corner pocket seams, either by the edge of the pocket or by the inner seam of the pocket, usually with four pins. Others chose to place it over the line, or partially over the line, allowing the pockets to blow free and dry better. Some of you like to fold it in half and pin along the formed straight edge, again allowing the pockets to blow free. Those with a high line hung the sheet from two pockets, letting it hang straight, the same as you would do with a flat sheet. This isn't very common because most of us do not have the luxury of such height.

Tip: If it is very windy, try pinning each flapping part together. Simply put a pin on each end to hold the sheet closed. This helps to prevent it from wrapping around the line.

Pillow cases (cotton/print): By reversing the pillow cases, you allow accumulated lint to blow free. Most hang a pillow case by the closed end with two pins and others of you like to hang it by the open end on just one side, allowing air to circulate. It is important you hang matching pillow cases side-by-side; do not mix and match unless they are all of the same colour.

Controversy arose when it came to hanging bedding. Some say it is important to hang each set together: for instance, a solid blue flat sheet, fitted sheet and pillow cases need to hang together on the line. Others of you tell me it is important to hang all the flat sheets first, then the fitted, and then the pillow cases. Regardless of which way you choose, try to keep the family together as much as you can.

Heavier bedding, such as blankets and spreads, hang over the line because of the added weight. Even the best of pins have their limits. Hanging over the line prevents items from falling off and pinning keeps them in place.

Towels (terry cotton/print): Everyone seems to agree about towels – hang them from the end. Many of you follow the conventional way of hanging the solids together, the prints together with the print facing you and, if they have tags, all the tags facing the same way. Some of you will hang the prints to face away from the sun to prevent fading. Taking this to another level, if you have a cup towel, for instance, with a meadow scene on it, make sure the meadow is hanging like a meadow should hang: keep the roots near the ground and the clouds in the sky.

If you've already picked up on the different ways people obsess about hanging their laundry, keep reading because it gets even more unbelievable. It was at this point in the interviews when I started to notice more people wanting to express their preferences. At first people were a bit timid but once they realized I was honestly and seriously interested in knowing all they knew about clotheslines, they eagerly started to share their insights.

At a couple of interviews, people actually repositioned themselves in the room in order to make sure they could hear me and I could hear them. You have to remember, some of these people were in their eighties and nineties and had an abundance of clothesline knowledge to share. They didn't want to miss a thing and neither did I.

People were starting to take this project a bit more seriously and insisted on telling me "how" and "why." They wanted other people to know, too. At this stage of the interviews, I began to note how surprised people were at some of their colleagues' decisions. Increasingly, people began to defend their position with the utmost conviction. After all, don't be ridiculous, obviously there has to be a very good reason for doing something the same way for years. Those reasons were beginning to unfold. In the back of my brain, I envisioned the threat of war, at the least, a civil uprising. However, as Winston Churchill said, "When you are going through hell, keep going." So, back into the basket I went for the next item, not knowing what may unfold.

DOUG VAN HEMESSEN PHOTO

Hand towels, cup towels, face cloths and dish cloths: All of you followed the same rules as the larger towel. They are one big happy family.

Odd hand towel (terry cotton/print): Here is where I wanted to start testing skill levels, so I pulled out an odd-shaped towel with a print on one side and a buttoned tab at the top (allowing you to fasten it to a cupboard door or whatever). This little item had people stumped, then after a few seconds, most of you decided you would hang it by the bottom with two pins. Second choice was by the unbuttoned tab with one pin and bronze medal holders opted to button it to the line using no pins.

Again, I decided to throw in a trick question. Holding up a cup towel, a dish cloth and a pair of underwear (all the same basic colour), I asked people if these items were washed in the same load. People hesitated before answering. Most of you were thinking, "Hmm . . ." In the end, those of you who don't said so, and the rest of you didn't answer. Most of us do wash all these items together (according to colour) and hang them on the line, but not necessarily on the line together. As I said earlier, some people like to do a linen line and others of us insure our undies are closest to the house or nicely hidden on a separate line.

Large Oval Lace Tablecloth (solid/cotton): People pondered over this too. About two-thirds of you wanted to hang it over the line with two to four pins because you didn't want it to stretch or to blow off, while the rest of you agreed to fold it in half and pin it lengthwise with two to four pins. There were a few who were unsure about hanging it on the line at all.

Small Oval Lace Doily (solid/cotton): Again, most of you agreed to hang it the same way as the oval tablecloth. The exceptions wanted to hang it with one pin from the end or lay it flat to dry in the house on a towel. A few people wanted to pin it along the fold with one or two pins.

That finished up the linens. One person asked me about curtains. I didn't have any with me, but the group rallied together and offered their advice. Here is what they said.

Curtains: Hang from the top, allowing them to blow freely – no folding, or placing them over the line, unless they are very heavy. Some curtains need to be dry cleaned, so make sure you check first.

Now we move onto articles of clothing. This is where a lot of discussion took place and a lot of secrets were revealed. Included with the information shared at the interviews I will also include what people e-mailed me or told me when I went to the doctor's office, the post office, the bank, the parking lot, the garage, the theatre. Wherever I was, there was someone nearby with a clothesline-related story. I listened to them all and appreciated all I heard.

DOUG VAN HEMESSEN PHOTO

Lined Cotton Work Pants (solid/flannel cotton): The vast majority of you agree upon hanging any type of pants by the back of the waistband with two pins. Of you, most hang them to allow the wind to blow through the pant legs. Many people believe pants dry better if they are hung inside out. The rest of you liked to hang your pants by the cuff, one or two pins per cuff. Some pinned with the cuffs open, others with the cuffs together.

I have to mention a gentleman I met on my first interview who silently participated by nodding his responses. When it came to hanging pants, he nodded "no" to all the "regular" ways and I was stumped. I asked him to explain his method of hanging pants and this is what I learned: "by the cuff with the leg seams matching," in other words, the inner and outer seams of the left leg and the inner and outer seams of the right leg were aligned so that two pins would hold the legs of the pants together, four seams matching. He was already being questioned by the group and before I had an opportunity to ask, "Why?" he replied, "Hanging that way lets the wind naturally blow a crease in them, making ironing easier." But of course!

Jeans (solid/cotton denim): Whichever method you chose for the lined pants, most of you chose the same for jeans: by the waistband with two pins. Some of you hang them inside out so they won't fade, again by the waistband with two pins, maybe three. A small number of you like to hang them by the bottom, matching the seams, knowing as the gentleman earlier said, it allows the wind to make a natural crease down the pant leg. One lady stretches and pins the pant legs like a V and hangs socks in between . . . not your typical approach and one that almost sent me into cardiac arrest.

DOUG VAN HEMESSEN PHOTO

Bibbed Overalls (solid/cotton denim): This item put me on virgin ground with countless people. Many had never hung overalls or coveralls on the line so weren't sure how they might do it. I ended up with four basic methods: the top two ways, either by the pant legs allowing the straps to hang down (unhooked) with two to four pins or by flipping the bib over the line and pinning at the waist. The next two most popular ways were flipping the back over the line and pinning at the waist or hooking the straps over the line with one pin on each strap. Another way was to hang at the waist over the line with two pins.

DOUG VAN HEMESSEN PHOTO

Shorts (solid/cotton with elastic waistband): Most everyone agreed to hang from the waist with two pins. It was about half and half as to whether you chose to hang with the waistband open or closed.

Long-Sleeved Shirt (solid/cotton): Most of you agreed to hang from the bottom (or the shirt-tails) with two pins. Some of you like the idea of pinning the shirt wide open with four pins. Others of you wanted to hang from the shoulder seams with two or four pins. If you hang your shirt in this manner, it was suggested to fold the collar inside to prevent fading. Very few wanted to hang from the collar. Remember the man who hangs his pants upside-down by the matched seams? He hangs his shirt by the collar with two pins, claiming it makes it easier to iron.

Long-Sleeved Shirt (cotton/print): Follows the same method as solid with the exception of facing the print away from the sun to prevent fading.

Short-Sleeved Shirt (solid/raw silk): About two-thirds of you hung from the shirt-tails with two pins, the other third pinned at the shoulders and only a couple of you wanted to hang by the collar. Some had concerns about putting silk on the line at all and said hanging it on a hanger inside would be best.

T-Shirt (cotton with print): Because this was cotton, some of you hesitated about hanging it on the line and running the risk the shirt may stretch. It was almost a split decision whether you hung by the bottom or by the shoulders. The other option was hanging the shirt over the line at the armpits and pinning with two pins. Those who took the print into consideration either hung it facing away from the sun or inside out.

T-Shirt (solid/polyester): This followed the same rules as the cotton T-shirt, with less hesitation.

Tank Top (solid/cotton/polyester blend): This too followed the same rule as the cotton T-shirt, with hesitation associated with stretching. Again, evenly divided in terms of hanging by the bottom or by the shoulder straps.

Tank Top (print/cotton with buttoned front): The big question about this item was whether to hang it buttoned, partly buttoned or unbuttoned. The debate rested with efficient drying while eliminating the need to iron. Half of you decided to hang from the bottom, unbuttoned and the rest from the shoulders, buttoned, or partially buttoned. Because of the print, many considered the fading issue and hung accordingly (away from the sun).

Short-Sleeved Sweater (solid/cotton with buttoned front): Cotton always presented concerns and this sweater caused deep thinking. Some of you played it safe and decided to lay it flat on a towel inside. Most who willingly chose to use the line wanted to hang the sweater over the line at the armpits and pin. Others wanted to hang from the shoulders using four pins to evenly distribute the weight. Few chose to hang from the bottom. All agreed to keep it buttoned to prevent stretching.

Long-Sleeved Sweater (solid/heavy cable knit): As with the short-sleeved sweater, the same problems arose and you followed the same solutions. More of you choose to avoid the line and dry inside on a flat surface.

Cardigan (solid/fine cotton): Most of you opted for the line with this sweater, mainly because it was more lightweight than the previous sweaters. A few still wanted to dry it inside, but the liners chose either by the shoulders with four pins and buttoned or from the bottom, buttoned, with four pins.

Tip: *If you are questioning "to button or not to button," the general rule is buttoning helps to maintain the original shape.*

Coat/Jacket (not actually in basket, used my own): The masses agreed to hang unzipped from the bottom with two or four pins. A couple of you wanted to straddle the coat over the line along the inner spine, if you will, using two or four pins.

Dress (solid/polyester): Almost everyone agreed to hang this dress on a hanger in the shower, primarily because it was quite frilly and very lightweight. The liners decided to hang it by the shoulders with two or four pins.

Sundress (cotton/print with spaghetti straps, buttoned down front): This little item caused some confusion, likely more for me than anyone. Many varied ways were being thrown at me. Under the armpits seemed to be the most popular, followed closely by the base of the straps, or by the straps themselves. Most agreed to leave the unit buttoned, or at least partially buttoned. Some thought by the bottom until I flipped it over and they discovered the bottom was like a flared skort. (Skort: n. *N Amer.* A pair of women's shorts for casual or semi-casual wear, with a flap of material draping the front, giving the appearance of a wraparound skirt – *The Canadian Oxford Dictionary)*

Long Skirt (solid/wool blend): Again, button, unbutton or on the line at all. This skirt was close to being evenly divided on all issues. Many chose to hang it inside. If you decided to hang it out, then you most likely hung it with two pins by the waistband, partially unbuttoned. If not, you likely hung it fully opened with four pins along the waistband. If you didn't fall into either of these three categories, you hung it fully opened from the bottom with at least four pins.

After all those tough decisions, things were getting a bit easier. Or were they?

Nightie (solid/cotton blend): This was evenly split, either from the bottom or from the shoulders, with two pins.

Housecoat (cotton/print): The most popular choice was by the bottom side-seams with two pins. Next popular was by the shoulders with two pins, and finally fully opened from the bottom with four pins.

Long Johns (solid/cotton): Almost all of you hung these by the waistband with two pins. Half of you wanted them pinned together and the rest pinned open. Only a couple chose to hang by the cuffs.

Everything seemed to be going along quite smoothly, but that was soon to change. Who would have thought socks and underwear (the best gifts ever) could cause such a controversy?

Socks (solid, print, mismatched or with holes): To begin with, most of you hung socks by the toe, either by themselves or in pairs. This was determined primarily by line space or pin availability. The rest of you hung by the toe, either together or singly and often for the same reasons. Some of you hung in pairs because it simplified the matching process. If, and heaven forbid it happen, you have an odd sock or a holey sock three options were available: hang them all together at the end of the matched pairs, mix them between matched pairs of similar colour and/or size, or, finally, don't hang them out.

This reminds me of a phone call I received late one evening from a woman who had spent a great deal of time tracking me down. When I answered, she frantically asked if I was who I should be. Once I confirmed that I was, you could almost hear her flop in her chair with relief. "I want to be in that book. I have a line of nothing but socks, white socks. One day I had seventy white socks on the line. People stop to look at my line." No doubt about that in my mind. Another tidbit of information you should know about hanging out your socks is to make sure they are all

Celestial Socks by Gloria Barrett, LaHave, Nova Scotia
(Acryllic and sparkle glue on canvas, 16 by 18 inches)

facing the same direction (all the heels facing the same way, for instance).

Also, remember to give them a good snap before you pin them. A friend of mine said she was told if you hold the sock by the toe and snap it, the sock will take on its natural form. For those of you who choose to hang all the socks together, most hang according to colour and/or size. Should you discover you are running short of line space, quite a few of you chose to hang the overflow over the laundry basket.

Panties (solid/polyester/cotton gusset): First of all, you either hung them out or you did not. This depended upon a number of factors. One lady told me, "When you get to a certain age, you start drying them inside." Another lady told me her daughter absolutely forbade her from hanging her undergarments on the line. May I note, this is the daughter of a devoted clothesline user. Other people told me the criteria for putting underwear on the line was based upon its size. "Once the panties reached a certain size, they couldn't go on the line anymore." Next, you either treated them like the rest of the gang, or you treated them more discriminately. Choosing the latter likely meant you placed them on the line in such a way that they could not be easily viewed.

Having all that established, the method you chose could be any of the following and I wouldn't be sur-

DOUG VAN HEMESSEN PHOTO

prised if there are more I have not heard of. If you will, play along. How many possible ways can you think of right now? Don't rush, I'll wait . . . Now, this may get to be a bit confusing, so pay attention. Basically, there were five different ways before we entered into the more eccentric possibilities.

Here is what I learned. First off, most of you hung your panties by the waistband, either open or closed with two pins. Second choice, hanging by the crotch with one pin. This method varied slightly. You either pinned at the middle of the gusset, you pinned along one of the gusset seams, or you hung the pantie partially over the line and pinned at the gusset. Thirdly, matching the side-seams and hanging by the waistband with two pins. Fourthly, hanging by the waistband in a kitty-corner manner. Another popular way is to hang your panties halfway over the line (either side-to-side or top-to-bottom) and pin with one or two pins.

More unusual methods include hanging along the side-seam with two pins, hanging upside-down by the leg openings with two pins and a three-way folded pantie hung from the waistband. Allow me to elaborate on the latter. If you lay a pair of panties flat, fold either side towards the middle so they meet (much like folding a formal letter) and hang. This should resemble hanging a legal-sized envelope by the short edge. One woman I met took this to the next level by folding the "legal-sized" pair of panties in half again, so now it resembled a square, and pinned it to the line using two pins.

Another lady told me her father used to hang panties all together. Not quite understanding what she meant, I asked her to explain. "Well, he pinned the first pair to the line, then pinned the next pair to that pair and so on."

"You mean they were all on top of each other?"

"No, the top of the second pair was pinned to the bottom of the first pair."

Got it! In case you missed it, they would look like rungs of a ladder. She said he usually got about four or five strings of them together.

Finally, all of the above methods are hung either inside out or right side out. Oh, I almost forgot, hang with all the bums facing the neighbours. There you have it. I have given you the options, you do the

At one time it was against the law in Kentucky to hang male and female underwear on the same clothesline. (DOUG VAN HEMESSEN PHOTO)

figuring. How many possible options can you figure out? (The answer is not found on any page).

Before I move on, we must address thongs. If you are unaware of what a thong is, simply put, it is the frame of a regular pair of panties with the buttocks and legs removed. I equate this to a rump roast where the fat and bone have been removed. Keeping with the lean theme, it does not mean cheaper, but it does mean fewer pins because there is so little to attach to the line. Chances are they may be dry before you even reach the line.

Boxers (cotton/print): Thank goodness for some normality again. All agreed to hang by the waistband with two pins, although some wanted just to pin along the back waistband instead of pinning it together.

Camisole (rayon/print): Most of you decided to pin this by the shoulders with two pins. Some chose the bottom, and others said they wouldn't hang it out-side. This may have been because some may have found it a bit risqué. I am not referring to the men.

At this point I would like to commend the men who participated. They were real troopers and none shied from the items I was displaying. I thought some may find the inclusion of undergarments offensive, but their participation demonstrated their commit-ment to help me with my project. Hats off to you, Gentlemen.

Bra (solid/cotton/polyester): Bras were straightforward (pardon the pun). Most chose to hang by the hook end with one pin. The next most popular was half-way over the line with one pin. The "not-at-all" people followed next. Only two people I interviewed hung their bras stretched fully, parallel to the line with a pin on each strap or upside-down using four pins. If you had a number of bras, some of you chose

to bunch them together, giving the illusion of a more solid item on the line. Others of you would hang two together.

Pantyhose (solid/polyester/rayon): Most people chose to hang pantyhose inside, but if yours managed to make it to the line, they likely found themselves hanging from the waistband with one pin. If not, they were hanging partway over the line with one pin. Only a couple of people hung from the toe, and only one pinned the waistband, then flipped the legs over the line, pinning them to the waistband, with a total of three pins. This was an attempt to prevent stretching. I met one woman who said she dries her pantyhose by wearing them (wet) until they dry. She claims the hose dries to the form of your legs. Don't ask me – I have not tried it.

Nearing the bottom of the basket were some miscellaneous items. These were for fun and to draw upon the knowledge of the true veterans.

Ball Cap (cotton/print): If you hang ball caps on the line, most of you hang from the back. Only one person pinned by the beak or brim. Others of you told me you place them over a bowl so they retain their shape or hang them on a door knob. Some people stuff caps with newspaper to help them hold their shape. The strangest I heard was washing and drying in the dishwasher. Yes, the *dish*washer. Sometimes innocence showed itself with comments like, "You can wash them?" One of the funniest answers I heard was from a woman who said, "Wash them? I just throw them out!" In baseball, the term clothesline refers to a ball hit straight and parallel to the ground.

Swimsuit (cotton/print): Like the cap, if you hang your swimsuit on the line, most did so by the straps. The next popular choice was by the gusset with one pin. A few people hung their swimsuit slightly over the line and pinned at the armpits or halfway over pinned at the trunk. Others of you choose to hang your swimsuit on a hanger in the shower. I am not sure whether all of you do this for the same reason, but one woman told me she won't hang swimsuits in the sun because they fade. As I write this staring out at the snow-covered, wind-swept field outside my window, I feel warm picturing the "vacation line" — nothing but brightly coloured swimsuits and beach towels dancing in the wind. Maybe the odd pair of shorts or wet sneakers hanging limply by their tongues, as if being scolded for having gotten their feet wet.

Gloves (solid/cotton): The number one best-selling method was to pin open by the cuff. Some chose pinning the cuff closed. Like socks, most of you decided to hang gloves separately. Unlike socks, gloves had to hang with the thumbs facing each other, the "natural" hand placement being important. A few people elected to pin gloves together, over the line. Although I didn't have any braces in my basket, I was told you would use the same hanging method. If you have an inside drying rack, sometimes people stick a glove on either end to dry. I have done this and while it works, the gloves cause an overall effect of total exhaustion. The rack looks as though someone has collapsed over it. I tire of watching them dry because I get worried they just might not make it.

Tote bag (print/blend): The last thing in my basket. I wasn't sure if people were getting tired at this point or whether I had actually stumped them, but this tote seemed to take considerably more time to resolve than I would have thought. Regardless, everyone rallied together and finished the race scoring high marks. Most people agreed to hang from the bottom with two pins. Others of you pinned open at the top corners and the remainder of you hung from the straps with one pin.

The basket lay empty before me, but my information recording sheets were overflowing. I think people thought I was done with them, but I wasn't. I wanted them to tell me *everything* about their line. I wanted to know their disaster stories, what else they have used their clotheslines for and if they had any tips for people.

We were off again, as the stories started to spill out and so did the laughter. Mixed among the laughs were groans when we heard of a downed line. It was especially amusing to listen to couples speak of their line. The his and her confessions – funny how a non-operable line suddenly becomes his or yours.

For a moment I want you to recall the beginning of our exercise. After I held an item up and you told me how to hang it, I placed it on the floor beside me and moved on to the next item. Over time the clothes developed into quite a pile. At the end of each interview I simply bunched everything together and rammed them, the best I could, into my basket and put the cover on. Upon returning home, I would remove each item, compare it to my records while the information was fresh in my brain and summarize my notes. On occasion, people offered to help me fold the clothes, though it wasn't necessary.

At the seniors home I visited, an elderly lady was sitting next to me and at the end of the interview when I started to haphazardly jam everything away, she kindly leaned over to me and whispered, "You really should learn how to fold, dear." I cannot say enough about how friendly and helpful people were. If smiles were dollars, I would be a rich, rich woman.

We all know old habits die hard. While I have discovered (now) that different hanging techniques may yield improved results, my brain remains programmed to believe it has to be done "traditionally." I am working on adapting, though to be perfectly honest with you, I'm only humouring myself. Maybe that appears to be a sign of weakness, I don't know, but I think you should try it, just for your own personal satisfaction.

Pick a day, approach the line with an attitude of complete disregard for stature and hang your clothes differently than you normally would. I know, I know, it is a lot to ask. Do it when you know your neighbours will be on vacation or when you are expecting company (and blame it on them). The point is, we should try an idea before concluding "the only way is my way." Oh hell, just do it for the fun of it!

5

Other Uses of the Line

If you thought the only use for a clothesline was for hanging your laundry, your predisposed belief is about to be challenged. Clotheslines have served as multifunctional tools for years. Fishermen and hunters have historically used lines to dry their codfish, eels, rabbits and other game. Lines were used to hang pelts and caches of food. Fishermen often hung nets over the line to dry and mend.

While in Newfoundland and Labrador this past summer, I had the unique pleasure of viewing some of these lines and being humbled. Seeing a fishnet hanging on a weather-worn line makes you feel insignificant, knowing the greatness it symbolizes. Hardship, love, and conviction radiated from those lines straight into my heart. I felt invigorated and tired all at once. For me it created a gamut of emotions, compelling me to revisit what is truly important.

In French Canadian cultures, it was tradition to hang a rosary on the line the night before your wedding to insure fine weather the next day. It would be interesting to know the success rate of this custom.

Like many others, you may like to hang your suet cages and bird feeders on the line. The idea is to keep the squirrels away from the feeder and while it makes sense, I have to wonder if it doesn't encourage birds to poop on your clothes. I have seen lines with the combination of feeders and laundry. I haven't tested this out and don't intend to. As my friend Tom would say of things he was disinclined to take on himself, this is a "good job for you."

Tom was a gentleman I cared for when I worked at King's Meadow Residence, in Windsor, Nova Scotia. He and I shared many common interests, but the favourite two were using the clothesline and fishing. Tom loved to fish and he was also quite methodical about his clothesline, making sure things were straight and orderly. Sometimes he was more interested in using the clothesline because he knew it would provoke someone who couldn't use it, giving him supremacy and great personal satisfaction. When he wanted something he could not attain on his own or didn't particularly feel like doing, Tom often responded with "good job for you." Tom has since

passed away. I think he would be glad to know I am writing this book.

My sister told me they used to hang rabbits on the line when she was a kid living on the farm. I am glad my birth occurred some years later.

I have seen a line adorned with stuffed animal toys. Coincidently, the toy line I saw was across the road from the farm my sister spoke of.

Another farm-related story, which I found extremely strange and, yes, somewhat disturbing, was hanging hens in a burlap bag to stop them from setting. The first time I heard this story, I was aghast. With some hesitation, I carefully asked the group if the hens were dead or alive, and with some surprise was told, "Well, alive of course," which horrified me even more.

"Well, how many did you put in a bag?" I asked.

"Only one, dear."

Still horrified I asked, "Well, how long do you leave them in the bag?"

"Overnight, but if they tried to set on their eggs again, back in the bag they'd go for another night."

"How many nights did it take?"

"Usually not more than two or three."

Another chicken story I heard went like this: "When I was a child, I visited my aunt and uncle on their small farm in Alberta in the early 1950s. It was chicken-killing day and much to my horror and dismay they fastened the luckless hens upside down to the clothesline and proceeded to slit their throats. It certainly gave new meaning to the term 'drip dry.'"

Clotheslines play an important role in rug beating. You hang your area rugs over the line and "beat the hell out of them." There is a special tool devised for this job which resembles a wire snowshoe on a handle, but commonly you would use a broom or paddle of some sort. This act combines two very important factors and should be encouraged more by mental health practitioners. It not only provides an essential service, but it is also a fantastic stress releaser. Many people still beat rugs in this manner.

Tip: You may want to approach this activity with caution as it may not be suitable for all listeners.

A line not far from our home always has a string mop hanging at the end of it. Logical deduction leads me to suspect the floor gets washed after the laundry is done . . . or maybe the washer leaks. Amazing what you can deduce from viewing a line. Your clothesline instantly reflects any household news.

Take this story for instance: "My first two children are very close in age and so I wore the same maternity clothes both times. Eighteen months of those same clothes made me so sick of them that after my second son was born, I took scissors to the outfits, removed all the buttons, washed and hung the pieces out to dry to use for rags. . . . After seeing me in those same clothes for so many months, my neighbours instantly recognized the rags. My phone rang off the hook. 'So, you've obviously decided not to have more children.' 'Two's enough?' 'New wardrobe being planned?'"

I have heard many stories about diaper lines and the warm feelings they incur. One hardworking woman told about purchasing disposable diapers (a novelty and expensive treat at the time) for her mother to use when caring for her newborn. She showed her how to use them and then headed off to work. Upon her return home, she discovered a row of seven disposable diapers hanging on the clothesline. "I washed them," her mother said. "They are so pretty it is a pity to throw them away!" This same woman told me about bringing home a very handsome friend only to discover her mother had her very large undies hanging on the line.

Another woman told me about an elderly neighbour relating a diaper recollection she had of her husband. He was out in the backyard on a step-ladder in a blizzard, using a hammer to free the drying diapers because they had blown up and over the top line and frozen in place.

A woman e-mailed me her reminiscence: "When I had three babies, I *loved* hanging out the cloth diapers on the line, and I loved looking at them, and smelling them when I brought them in to fold! The significance was: it was like an announcement that this house had a baby, and being very environmentally conscious, the other message was cloth diapers make sense/cents!"

Diaper lines are not as common now, but you can still find them and I agree, they are beautiful to look at. Like fresh sheets, diapers have a special feel and smell that only air drying provides. The sterilizing effect of the sun is amazing.

This woman shares her thoughts on the line next door. "There was an abandoned but tidy older house near us which has now been torn down. The lawn was always cut and one white tea towel was always hanging on the clothesline. We used to imagine that someone came and cut the lawn, had a cup of tea, washed and dried the cup and saucer and hung the towel on the clothesline."

You may be lucky enough to find lines housing bunches of flowers, herbs, or beans hanging until dried to perfection. On the other hand, you may be luckier to find plastic bags, maybe "Sunny Bee bread bags," drying on the line. The first sliced bread I can remember came in a plastic bag with a big black and yellow bee splashed across it. As a child, that bee was a sign that told me I didn't have to go through the agony of cutting homemade bread that never fit in the toaster the right way. If I chose, I could have perfectly formed sandwiches in my lunch. Frugal types would wash and dry the bags for future use. Many times I remember walking to school wearing a pair of Sunny Bee bread bags over my socks when I had forgotten to dry my boots the night before.

How about actually hanging bread on the line? This story was sent to me from Don: "My dad used to buy a dozen or so round loaves of Joululimppu Christmas bread from the Kivela Bakery. It was a dark rye with fennel and caraway seed . . . and was only baked at Christmas time. Mom would put each loaf in a pillow case and pin it to the clothesline. We could tell how much Christmas season was left by checking the number of bags left on the line." Joululimppu is pronounced yolualimpoo and is a Finnish sweet/sour bread. Each loaf fit perfectly into a pillow case and was hung on the line to freeze fresh. In Don's words, "You would only need to bring in one loaf at a time, so one loaf/pillow case worked nicely."

Tip: Please recycle whatever, whenever, you can.

I am told soldiers in World War Two would look at the clotheslines in small communities when searching for billets. It was suggested they find a household with a broom outside the door because this indicated a clean homeowner and a warm welcome. Apparently, the soldiers thought otherwise. They preferred to keep their eyes out for clotheslines with silk slips, and such for an even warmer welcome.

Campers like to hang their tarpaulins on the line to dry before putting them away for the season. After a downpour, you may find many nylon tents over the line. The same can be said for plastic bed sheets and sleeping bags.

Following along with the outdoor enthusiasts, using your clothesline as the official volleyball or badminton net is most honourable. I tried this as a child but the location didn't allow for maximum return possibilities. We should have gone to the neighbour's . . . when they weren't home.

As another purpose, people have been known to use the clothesline as a run, whether it is for your dog, your cat, your horse, your sheep or even your child. By affixing your rambunctious little one to the line with a harness and a long lead, you can prevent your precious possession from escaping the backyard. I know there are a number of you who will take offense to this tactic, especially with regards to children. I am not suggesting it is a safe practice to be followed by all. I am relaying what people told me they used to use their lines for. I think you should use whatever means available to insure the safety of your children with trusted supervision of paramount importance.

Another unique use also needs a word about safety. Some of you like to hang your hammock from the line. Having never tried this myself, *test* with the utmost of safety in mind. Depending upon the amount of activity in the hammock, you might want to restrict this application.

My sister referred to her husband's attempt to move firewood from the adjacent barn into the house by hooking up a transfer system via the clothesline. It didn't work. The concept simply required more refinement.

That reminds me of another story told to me about an aunt living at the foot of the hill below the niece's family home. She used the clothesline to pass the newspaper up the hill, eliminating the need to walk back and forth in bad weather. The aunt, however, could never quite understand why the system needed two pulleys if you were only sending the paper in one direction.

There are those of you who like to hang flags on the line, Halloween decorations at the end of October, or Christmas lights during the holiday season. Until my husband made us a flagpole, I used to hang the flag on the clothesline on Canada Day.

While these are all very picturesque, nothing is more breathtaking than a line displaying homemade quilts. These lines are stunning, artwork upon artwork.

Some of you like to use your clothesline as a privacy fence, hanging blankets to keep outsiders from looking in. The reason you use blankets instead of sheets is because blankets are heavier and move less. Sheets on the line will flutter and move much easier.

One of the cleverest uses, I thought, was as a watch dog. If you know your neighbour is going away for an extended period of time, you (acting assistant) will either make a point of moving your neighbour's line back and forth and changing what is on it to indicate they are home, or else you simply put your laundry on their line. (Suddenly, I feel as though I have betrayed my followers. Rest assured, the bad guys still don't know.) An active line indicates someone is home. I thought this was the ultimate alternative use. Don't ever underestimate the power of clothesline operators – they are constantly planning their next move.

6

Clothesline Mishaps

Originally, I was planning to call this chapter "Clothesline Disasters," but many of the stories people told me were very amusing and quite entertaining and I didn't want to appear to be associating humour with disaster.

Anyone who has suffered a downed line will attest there is in fact nothing funny about it. However, those who have witnessed the process may say it is very comical.

This story comes from a woman who obviously loves her husband very much: "I had the clothesline *full* with clean clothes when my husband attempted to go under it with his farm tractor and guess what?! Clothes all over the yard and dragging with him and the tractor. Well, you couldn't help but laugh! I didn't really enjoy picking up the clothes, rewashing them and waiting to fix the line so it could be used again."

Whenever I conducted an interview with couples and I asked if anyone had ever had a downed line, inevitably the woman would yell yes, and turn to her husband, who would already be hanging his head. It made me laugh to see this repeated at other interviews. Reasons why the line fell in the first place varied. What didn't change were the accusing looks. At times the blame game came into play. "You hung too damn much on it" or "If you had gotten a new pulley instead of trying to fix that broken one, this wouldn't have happened." Seems an operating line belongs to *her* and a downed line belongs to *him*.

Initially, when I asked people to tell me their clothesline "disasters" the most common mishap was when the line broke . . . full of clothes. Inevitably, the clothes would end up in the mud or wet grass. Someone told me their line stretched over the backyard pool and when it broke, well, you get the picture.

I have experienced this most dreaded occurrence and relate it to the big blue screen which shows its evil face on the computer just before it rudely announces it is shutting down, just before you hit "save." It makes me feel sick. Now, that should be referred to as a disaster.

Chris had fixed the pulleys on my line about a month earlier and all was grand; my line was quieter, faster and more streamlined than ever before. It gave me that new car feeling – it was great. I had a very important engagement to attend on Sunday morning, and decided to hang my white wash out Saturday night. That way, I could have it dried and off by the following noon.

Sunday morning was beautiful, and before rushing out, I decided to grab my towel and swimsuit off the line, thinking a leisurely swim would go nicely before I returned home. Reaching up, I yanked the two off the line and that's when my world stopped.

Actually, it fell. The entire line came down. My fifty feet of white wash was lying across the yard. The sheets were in the flower garden, my clothes were in the vegetable garden, the cup towels were spread over the pathway, and my undies were lying across the bayberry bush. And you know, my line didn't care . . . it just lay there, not making a move. Not a sound could be heard, nothing. Not even an attempt at an apology.

I stood there in utter astonishment. "No," I thought, "this can't be happening to *me*!" I looked around to see if anyone else had seen what happened, but the coast was clear. I quickly snatched my camera and photographed the crime scene. "No one will believe this," I thought. After some brief ranting, what could I do but laugh. I rapidly began to unpin each damp piece lying on the ground and toss every-

thing into the basket until I returned. It was getting late and I had to hurry off, knowing full well what faced me when I came back.

The following true story was sent from Stuart Houston who recalls how great our "Greatest Canadian," Tommy Douglas, *really* was.

Picture a small cottage on the Saskatchewan Prairies in the early 1940s, where a devoted daughter lives with her aging mother. Stuart recalls, "A fastidious nurse by training and a loving daughter, my Aunt Mary would change the bed sheets a number of times each day, keeping Granny clean and dry at all times.

"The year was probably 1944, the year that Douglas won a landslide victory and became premier, the first social democratic (socialist) premier in North America.

"Tommy, as everyone called him, drove alone to Tyvan. He wished to visit my Aunt Mary and Granny in the hope of gaining their votes for his CCF [Cooperative Commonwealth Federation] candidate. He drove in the back lane, and drove across the parched grass right up to the back door of my Aunt Mary's little cottage.

"The entire clothesline, forty feet or more of it, was filled with the morning's wash, literally out to dry in the prairie sun. Heavy sheets formed a disproportionate amount of the washing.

"Just as Tommy stopped, a massive gust of wind came through the yard. The large post that held the end of the clothesline adjacent to the cottage began to crack audibly near its midpoint. Tommy saw that, if the upper half of the post fell over, all the wash would soon be in the dirt. Without hesitation he leaped out of his car, bounded up the step or two behind the cottage to the platform where Aunt Mary had stood when she had pinned the sheets on the line with clothes pegs. Just then Aunt Mary came to the nearby cottage door. Tommy held the partially broken post high enough to keep the sheets above ground while Aunt Mary quickly unpegged them from the clothesline and put them in a basket. Every item of the large wash was saved."

Who says politics don't have a place on the line?

I remember a lady telling me a clothesline story about a young bride and her husband moving to the country to live with his parents on the family farm. One day the young bride did the laundry and hung it out to dry, anticipating no problems. It was haying season and her father-in-law was coming out of the fields with a wagon full of hay when he noticed the line of clothes across his path to the barn. It was very hot, so he decided to stop and take a break. Upon entering the kitchen he noticed his new daughter-in-law had brewed a fresh pot of tea. He calmly remarked, "I wouldn't mind a cup of that and would you please take your clothes down."

One day while I was getting tires put on my car, the conversation swung to my book (surprise!). I heard the mechanic working on the car next to mine say, "Nothing sweeter than sheets fresh off the line. Nothing better than that." When you hang your laundry out expecting it to come in smelling fresh, it is always a disappointment when it doesn't. Discovering you are downwind of a dead skunk, a fire, or emissions from local industry can have undesirable side effects. Placing a scented dryer sheet on the line will not prevent your wash from absorbing unpleasant aromas.

Animals are not without their day in court. Dogs insistently tug at hems until finally freeing your best white linens, and then drag them through the mud in preparation for the next wash day.

One particular dog I know likes to chew my prop. Having your prop pulled out from under you is not a good thing. You can well imagine a prop line without a prop just isn't proper.

And what about cows that wander out of the pasture? How is it they automatically head straight for the clothesline? With broad shoulders and horns held

high, they march forward ever so calmly, and strip your line of every sheet and pin. The beasts may stop temporarily to admire each other's work before parading through your yard and into the neighbour's for a repeat performance. Inevitably, escapees will end up wearing your clothes. Size and style are irrelevant.

Squirrels and chipmunks like to steal soft items for nesting material. Birds with bodily urges may leave unpleasant streaks on your laundry. You are not apt to discover this until you have reached the folding process, in which case what might have been only one item with bird poop on it, you have managed to turn into about seven items.

Bees can be a real problem. Make sure your clothesline area is free of any small holes which have the potential to provide a safe haven for these stinging hymenopterous insects of the genus *Apoidea*. Because bees are attracted to your white laundry, and they colonize, make a serious effort to dissuade them from setting up housekeeping in your backyard. (Contributed by those formerly stung.)

Bugs. Pick a bug, any bug, and someone has likely found it in their bedding or underwear. Insects are infamous for entering households via the clothesline. Ants climb along the line as if it were a super highway, clean, clear, and straight to their destination. Others prefer to be carried into the house via the basket of fresh laundry.

Tip: Give each item on the line a good sharp snap before you put it in your basket. This will shake out any attached bugs . . . I hope.

The frozen line – the one where nature has permanently affixed the clothes to the line – has to be one of the most challenging. Removing frozen clothes is not an easy feat. Instead of risking frigid fingers, many people just leave them there until they thaw. The more adventurous among us will pry them off the line and stack them like slices of bread, lug them into the house, and try our best to thaw them, only to hang them back out the next day if they are still

Snow by Gloria Barrett, LaHave, Nova Scotia
(Acryllic on canvas, 16 by 18 inches)

damp. Speed is the key when hanging in sub-zero temperatures. If you are not quick, you end up with a basket of frozen fibre. On the other hand, I have seen some lines where the steam is rising from every item. Now that is fast!

This is a funny story about a woman who kept receiving phone calls from an unknown caller. The stranger kept asking her if she had a fax line. Out of sheer frustration, the woman finally told the caller, "I don't know what you are talking about. All I have is a clothesline!" and hung up. The calls stopped coming.

Another lady said when she was a child, she was watching her brothers playing with a BB gun. The boys had mounted a target on the tree that supported the clothesline. She wanted to play too, so she asked if she could have a turn. Her brothers thought they would humour her and give her one try. When she fired, she hit a clothespin on the clothesline. Of course, her brothers were amazed at what a good shot she was – to be able to pick off a clothespin at that distance was good. She never told them she was aiming for the tree.

We have all heard about clothes blowing off the line, some to be found and some never to be seen again. One lady noticed she was short a pillow case. She looked for it, but could not find it. She sent her boys in search of the missing case, but they couldn't locate its whereabouts either. The following spring, there it was, across the field, high in a tree. It had wintered all alone in that tree, waiting to be rescued.

A woman who had just moved into a new neighbourhood brought in her laundry, only to discover she was missing a black negligee. She was unable to find it on her own and was too embarrassed to inquire as to where it could be. A few days later, a knock came on the door. When she answered it, the gentleman standing there held up her negligee and asked, "Is this yours?" Handing it back to her, he smiled and said, "I found it in my yard and knew it didn't belong to my wife."

In a different rural community another black negligee went missing. Only this time, the farmer's daughter found it in the field and came knocking on the door, inquiring as to where it may live. The lady of the house was rather embarrassed when she took possession of her lost nightie. Wonder how many doors the young girl knocked on before she found the right one?

This lingerie line (specifically baby dolls with matching panties) was in full view of the general store where the husband of the hanger worked. Later that day, a local elderly man from a nearby village came into the bank where she worked and announced that he had just visited the country store and he declared to all, that "Judy, you have the prettiest clothesline in town!" She claims her husband was more embarrassed than she was.

It is one thing to have items blow off the line, but another to have things stolen. This story comes from a gentleman who lived in Malawi, Africa. It is about his friend Jim, who taught school for sixty years. Jim's clothesline was made of galvanized single strand steel wire, because fibre lines rotted due to the high humidity. Here is his story: "My friend Jim grew tired of having his clothing stolen. He understood that the local population perceived him as being immensely wealthy and therefore would never miss the occasional item of underwear or socks, but it was becoming a nuisance to send to South Africa or Europe for replacements. So he hit on a scheme to end the pattern of behaviour.

"The first stage of the project involved the construction of a red light which flashed whenever line voltage was applied to the circuit. It was simply a flashing light which was mounted inside a house window, in full view of anyone near to the line. He then loosened a patch of soil beneath the line and after driving a long metal peg into the centre of the patch, he poured a strong brine solution around the peg to make a perfect ground connection.

"A thin copper wire was connected from the line to the peg in the ground and 220 volts was connected through a switch, so that when the switch was activated, the voltage would be applied to both the flashing light and the clothesline simultaneously – but the switch was *not* closed at this time.

"Jim then called his houseman, his gardener and the night security guard and any other curious onlooker who could be persuaded to see the demonstration. He stood them at a safe distance from the line with strict instructions to venture no closer. And then Jim closed the switch.

"The red light started to flash and the thin copper wire glowed white hot before it vapourized and disappeared with a bang and a puff of smoke!

"The demonstration was most effective.

"Of course, Jim disconnected the electrical supply to the line permanently, but left the flashing red light in the window, giving his houseman strict instructions to have the light (and the non-existent power to the line) turned off before he ever touched the line again. No more underwear ever went missing!"

Another embarrassing clothesline moment happened to a friend of mine who had recently moved north. One day, she got her bra caught in the pulley at the far end of her second story clothesline (no, she wasn't wearing it at the time). Not knowing anyone in the building, or the community for that matter, she called her husband at work and told him her predicament. He arrived home after work with a crew he had rallied together and the rescue was underway. I am happy to report the mission was a success and she quickly became well known in the community.

Other people have similar stories of sheets wrapping around their line at twenty-five feet in the air. Understandably, recovering these can be quite an adventure and involve a select vocabulary. Remember in the old westerns when the shoot-out at sundown was about to take place and all the townsfolk ran for cover? You may consider being a townsfolk if you're not part of the problem.

A solid line can knock a sturdy man right off his feet, off his horse, off his motorcycle or off his bike. Accidents do happen and are not funny, though you have to chuckle when a poor soul gets up and is stunned by what just happened. As one man said, "Hanging from the chin outdoors improves your memory, although doing little for the ego."

While most of these anecdotes are harmless, I would be remiss if I did not remind you to keep your fingers clear of pulleys or other moving parts. Getting your fingers pinched hurts, it really hurts.

The Final Peg

You can follow any line to its maturity by simply watching the changes that occur over years of use. Your line indicates growth, lifestyle and values. Reflections of life are time-honoured through the preservation of our heritage and traditions. Your clothesline reflects your life.

A number of wonderful people throughout this project have shared their stories and knowledge. They have stepped up to the task and proven their expertise. You would expect this over years of using a clothesline.

I was surprised and delighted to see how attentive children are to clotheslines. "My mom hangs all the towels together. She puts the big ones first." It became clear that traditional traits were being instilled in these young minds. Isn't that comforting? By examining their art work and reading their stories, we are reassured that they are learning and appreciating clothesline traditions. With another proud generation of liners growing in society, this important part of our culture will be preserved.

Thanks

Special thanks goes to photographer Doug van Hemessen and artist Gloria Barrett. Doug lives near Owen Sound, Ontario, and his work can be found on his website – www.dvh.ca. Artist Gloria Barrett has a studio/gallery in LaHave, Nova Scotia.

To all the children who helped me with my project, thanks. Every picture and every word meant something very special.

The people I met over the course of this project were so enthusiastic and supportive, I want to make sure they know how much I appreciate their efforts. While I cannot possibly mention every name, you decide which category *you* fall into.

Thanks to
those who participated in my interview process,
all the individuals who e-mailed, wrote or called,
CBC Radio and Television,
friends,
neighbours,
my family,
and
especially, those who design their lines day, after
day, after day.

A Tribute

I feel the need to mention another special influence that played an important role in my fulfilling this dream. My dad passed away just at the beginning of this project, and while he was not here in body to help guide me through what he would say "needed to be done," his spirit seemed to help the winds blow success in the right direction.

I offer this tribute to my dad. He was a great storyteller and always loved the gift of laughter. He didn't display any outward affection, but he didn't need to. Maybe that sounds mean to some, but to me it meant he knew that I knew what I was doing. It was somehow reassuring to know he trusted my judgment. Through carefully chosen words, he was able to instill in me a set of values and principles that I can be proud of.

In my former line of work, it was mandatory to complete an annual job evaluation. One question on the form always troubled me: "How can you improve your work performance?" I found that question exasperating because I was raised with a work ethic of doing your best *every* day. Isn't that just common sense? Sometimes a basic understanding of expectations is worth more than any wordy lecture. Unless there was a story worth telling, Dad didn't say too much.

I must relay a story Kathy told about her clothesline and my dad. Kathy and her husband Mark were especially generous neighbours and our family is very grateful to them. One day, Dad drove in their yard and went to the door to tell Kathy her line of clothes had fallen. Kathy, naturally, hustled off to attend to the calamity. Not long afterwards, the same thing happened with the same chain of events taking place. Finally, a few months later, on a cold wintry day, Dad drove in the yard again. She went outside to see what he wanted and from the car window, he shouted, "That god damn line broke again!" A finer line has never been spoken.

I love you, Dad, and really miss you.